The Obedient Door

Sean Tumoana Finney

Meritage Press • St. Helena and San Francisco, California

Acknowledgements

Some of these poems are published in O-blek, Lingo,
        The San Francisco Bay Guardian, and Viz.

Book design and production by Ward Schumaker and Lori Barra.

Meritage Press books are published by Eileen Tabios who
        thanks "Oenophiles for Poetry" for their support.

Meritage Press logo design by Theresa Chong.

ISBN-13: 978-0-9709179-4-2
ISBN-10: 0-9709179-4-5

Meritage Press
256 North Fork Crystal Springs Road
St. Helena, CA 94574

www.MeritagePress.com
MeritagePress@aol.com

www.stfinney.com
www.warddraw.com

for my parents

CONTENTS

The Obedient Door

House of Leaves

Jealous Years

The Original Lyric

Secrets on Call

The Obedient Door

Shout Words at Your Feet

Our deep green descent
of the lake road
in arms again and after
nothing to turn away

from the syllables on a different
autumn road, where I watched the leaves
shout words at your feet

Shelve the past, its mullions,
its cardinals, rent from their homes
on cold streets

and to design you, out of glass,
no one sat

Actually We'll Never Know

I could mention cars
and bricks and streets retreating.
You might mention leaves. No,
I would mention leaves.
You would mention something I would not expect,
like that man's hands and this strange stone.

I would mention a lot of things in a series
to try and get the feeling of speech
rolling. Because actions don't quite match up,
their thumbs opposing in an entirely
different way than how words
click each other off.

But it was speech, and I will miss it because
some nets we've thrown to drown the squirmers
flop where we want them.

Can you see now how hard it is
to find the language that we'll never know?

Rocking back on our heels to celebrate
        the weaving we've accomplished
the light is strong and scintillates the backs of trees.
Shaved under my head in invisible ink the word
No.

Which the Leopards Reject

which the pile of thoughts wrestle
which the ends ignore and which
is of a high place that makes
water for the place where time
is spent carrying water and
a precarious time is wet
with questions (about the heights). Songs
nap in the shadow of a rocking hand

which song brings stones' rise and waters' fall
into the bending of wrists and ankles
and broken corners for dust to change light
into a way out of everything works
and is mixed without scent and dries

which poverty means staring
at hot milk and instant coffee
at burning little things and sun
and snow piled up

feel the rooms above the archway
talk from wooden shades where
the foil of afternoon snacks
contains the feelings of these rooms—
their taste for exile

Land is a plot where longhairs
remember and make it into books.
Books are lotteries of numbers
for the doors above the courtyard,
leisure between three and four
in the old world
behind wooden shades
with the "A" for apartments
and the doorway between the legs
that is up and to build the polite
hours of misunderstanding
as the wish for favorite foods
sprinkles consciousness
that is a river of protected thumbs
in pockets (there's no food without pockets).
Shy is the regular always finding
above the conversation gulf
that invites the sunlight of skinned knees
of I've forgotten to be so when the bell
intones for left-handed scissors
and silent vowels that ring
excuses to remember

and somebody needs to know what you're doing
that's why the early dialectic in hand tools
contained a hunch about the future.
It was impossible to stop, wasn't it?
When the bell intoned for a new grouping
you were ready with your bandaged sign language
of the left out that groaned in its paper cup.
"The sun will melt wax
and face every eye with the appeal to be still
and not listen to the until-next-week
satisfaction of cooperating."
Be a puddle or a line of shade
move like water or a table
and gently scratch the cliff of being taken care of

Along the River

Surface where boats will sport the nerves and crannies
undoing the vine
lurch the summer months
is thin the veneer
where boats will lurch
mouths gone, and the sparkle
of leaves caught in the air.

Ocean, your part too
revealed by the boat
chugs its stencils of people
for a gasp in the river.

Why, poor tree, are you not dressed?
Upon the bend is doubt
of bare arms flip in the wind.
Spring is come up upon the river.

Too slow for you, dance of
telephone wires.
The train is the rocks against
placed in the hill.
The bright lights of the fair
away in the dark,
Sharp flower of the ferris wheel.

By a yellow lamp a tree bends.
In the river leaves
clot by a stick.

On That Gnomelike Bench You Sat

In her arms
on the known vowels
pushing ice designs

three wheat weeds said they
were the sun
depressed into summer.

Do you feel the steps
are benches
for history, bright afternoon
in the Circus Maximus?

I was just on a quest
for hashish. The jealous god
of the air has rights.

Rome, two days of ochre and red, he wrote.

There was no sequence of destinations.
There were no sequin destinations,
no two cymbals
that never competed
in the line of a dress.

This is winter in summer,
the silhouette of a tailor
needles in his teeth
cutting the sun
into winter ribbons
renewed in the cold air.

China Desires a Wild Time

"Would you like two concubines or one? And
when you die will you reward her with the green
axe head? The special one."
The Spring and Autumn Annals

Seems silly some of these furrows
grown mounds of city seems silly
all the time we spent getting here.
Pegged out a few jostles of track and the difficulty
of the ticket. Hot tea spilled and mopped in the train
woman's routine.
I am confronted by the Gansu horse and it of course
is green.

(Could you flow your hair like that horse maybe
running Ferghana of hair all patched in the dark.)

Do you know these horses
and do you know the princess
they sent out to the Nomads
for a few?
Died in a smelly tent
It seemed my China breathed her last.

I don't think it was the sand swept breadth
of the thing, all hoary angles
some last blemish of wall
composed in a corner of where empire did stretch.
I don't think it was the mist on the hills
or the way the saddle rubbed her raw but
have you seen the poems scratched in the last gate
some spidery literati's hand waving her on
its brick one among many the horse bolted
sand crept up my princess's arm.
At night no street steam spoke for late pleasures,
Cold moon, Camel's head
Can you believe it now?

Pharos

Dogmatic city of ruined lights
that haunts the Greek infiltration
of all my baths, your face
corroded like a coin

and the careful belt you won
in a fair and wore
(legend interweaving)
to my wedding—
that's senescence under
the original hut

that's the senescence of a snake
eating itself.

[now the 75-year-old diver is eager to resume her investigation]

Neoprene nights amassed like days.
You'll believe the creeping love of red chairs
is real
and beaten out of copper.
[past tense, lighting tricks]
Handsome underwater archeologists
have gotten over their names
and the injected clouds.

I sat mapping the red stones
that will grow your hair.

Kings blister from the dour water of selling.
There is a tureen of hate in your stare
from greed eaten according to menus of grey skies
that are pants in every other language.

Stone for Courting

Perfect bliss greeted a leopard's family
and each lover worshipped
the half dozen doors favored

Under those wire balconies
this hope ran like a long sentence
yes yes yes no
I smell the brakes
on their sea chant course

These hills, not your hills
Agreed, and sensitive
clamor

Winter Snippets

house, shower, unknown
reason for being

noise, water, honking
the bridge

house, change, yards
of season, keening
marsupial we desire

give me so many days of sun

● ● ●

earth lights shadow
and palms season their union
with bridges of thick paper
turned from cattle
to cotton thought flavored
I'll be sick forever
in your estimation skiing

Toes Carved Out of Butter

I wish I had a notebook to write these lies in. Then when the slaves
kissed you they could carry it in their free hands, all six victims of plan-
ning nestle while the train
goes overhead.
      This dirty ruled paper is indebted to both of my worlds.
      I lived in a house of leaves where you cooked antique recipes.
      The snow kept coming in the background. It was more viscous
than television or sleep deprivation.
      You followed me when I was studied and when I was happy.
The deprivation used moments to get at your eyes. I cried impossible
smile deduct points from free hands.

Now I'm in a Chicago apartment
plastered with books.
They've been the problem you know.
Your hands work underground and
there's no copying anything.

You removed my belief in trembling
drunk osmosis with a woman.

Why do these wheels tediously break spirit?
Why don't they spin with such great noise
that the slaves wake and drown me
in humid air?
I never saw a waist
without asking god for a paper shield
great enough to charge.

• • •

You're angry, purple with prestige.
Gaps in the air,
all harmonized tweed
in the eucalyptus.
Renowned principle of disassembly
your entrée is behind a numbed door.

The red wall needs art
as much as the yellow.
I sentenced art to gladness
without hammers or clocks
that run bitterly
like fond leeches on stairways
like a hand on your face to check
snow-melted lessons.

Tonight is buoy time
clanging the sea ends or the land ends
fix the horizon these late intentions anyhow.

Right out of the shower fresh
and rested from public transportation

Cats in the light from chairbacks
to linger on

• • •

It's probably spring
is what I hear cascade from the orifice of goats
that made your shoes.
What is his contribution
beyond the hang glider that says weekend
along the tongue-wet road?

• • •

I borrow a book about the gaze.
Underwear can't be changed.
In these Lilliputian episodes
I'm demeaned by the clock in the kitchen
that controls the food
and ticks with possibility,
three episodes deferred.

I embrace the city with toes carved out of butter.
The world's biggest air conditioner leans east
and gives slices of cake to the homeless.

A glass of crazy glue and we have a deal
and a welcome mat and a sundial magazine.

House of Leaves

Hawaii Fragments

The answer is salt, wet eyed,
no answer. You'll create
the wind in your mouth
for nothing. Jealousy is such a wind

In the shade
the lesson grows

we're apart too often
the garden is yes sir no sir

use the other side of the street
and devour your union

It's hard to be alone
and the point is to keep others
from being alone
your children question

• • •

To blink at someone
with those eyes.
Posture cannot save you.
It's egregious love
that waves like new boots.
Answer me by being
a prostitute. I'll stay still
while you roll in spaghetti

Beyond hair
more energy than the ocean permits
to escape. A park with major flowers,
the sun saying no no no, repetition
is wrong. It's along the fence of never
hate that the answers begin

(everything destroyed like an architect, bullet
train whistle through the window,
Japan, land of the long shoe horns
you can't remember)

• • •

This cold house

still I'm confident of you
reduced to comments
on a picture in a museum

Yes, I'm talking about her.
The never with a fence
and a message to create pleasure
on the other side. I don't care about
your speech, your pants,
your shoes. No handbag
to empty in the gutter.
The color doesn't matter.
Stupid underwear you screamed over.
That door is shut. Your words night soil.

I don't know anyone but you.
Is that better?

Rimbaud Poems

Fair Enough

The vision with all its airs.
Villa rumors, the soiled shell
of the troubadours.
Assist you. The arrests in life—O Rumors
and Visions.

Innuendo Feces

The vampire that rends us gently
commands that we amuse ourselves
and forget every receptionist.

Roll out the blouses, pair them with
an assault on the sea. For supplies
take the clothes you died in.

"Later that evening we needed to have a talk."

Reverse the command for the pond
under clouds for the filthy day.
Do you want me to write about you?
Each day quelled the last.
I fixed the same door until the lock
did not speak.

Row Out

"My friends, I see her waist as my own."
"I want to be queen."
She ranted and trembled.
He spoke with his friends
of revelations, terminal epaulets, island
husks noisy on the ground.

Pupil-tired was she of my guts for ambition.

A Une Raison

A ten digit coup on the tangerine
discharges the sons and begins a new harmony.

Your first step, it's a levee for men
to leer in papier-mâché.

Your head detours for a new love twice.

"Change our lots, cripple our fleas, and
prune time," chant the infants. "Elevate but
don't import the substance of our fortunes
and our eyes,"
they hurriedly conclude.

The arrival of the troubadours
who put out irises.

Veillées

I

Definitely resting, no fever, no lassitude
Open your pipe to the predawn sea.

There's friendship without ardor or foibles. Friendship.

II

The two extremes of the room, other décor of the conquest,
trapped beyond judgment. The carved wall
is a succession of psychological blows, snobberies,
the cold air of geological accident—
rapid and intense dream of sentimental groups
constructed from white ash.

III

The sea is ugly, tell it to the dawn of silk
(tell it to someone's breasts).
The tapestries, midlevel, show factories for dentists
tinted with emerald, or the jettison of cake makers
who are ugly.

Cabin of Logs

She sits with dark patches
saying turn me

I'll see you and be pleased
as a light hidden under blankets
is inflated with borrowing.
There's so much of that
congealed in the calendar.

This is the preparation ad nauseam:
a pile of logs to burn the seat
of a tiny king who clings
to a telephone composed of mist.
I never understood that date,
the point where my umbrella felt like a cane.
Did you wear underwear to scream over?

The waiting game I haven't told you about
is contingent on waking, dressing, dining
giving answers to how you look
in every corner of the elevator.
There's no waist anymore.

Delayed for long slow periods by a blanket
we drink the same heated cider.
Each room listens for the stone roads
to be deposed.

Brassai

Brassai
is an eyebrow
a suspiration
for the sun
that we received

When I was 11
airports made me happy.
You'll smile at this,
"made me happy"
as if it's so fantastic
to buy ice cream
wear trousers, etc.
Keep up with the
acrid chemical sun

Sticks lashed to make a fence
cheaper and more beautiful
in my numbness—
that one machine for denying night

Brassai, you don't have
any memories

Four o'clock, great chill,
promise of drunkenness
Allison pissed on the street
Her friend demurred

History grows weeds in the sun
I never cried in the Circus Maximus

or kept my old promises
to the palm trees
to make them grotesque to foreigners

• • •

Postscript for Braque

When you're old and you paint a white bird
that's the limit.
There are hairs in every window
if you can walk.

Balthus

Balthus opens the window
with light arms and exclaims,
"Happenstance is the shovel."

Swarming measures suit the brown
and green pistachios

lost decades of slobbering
where the helmeted stand measuring beds

with empire feet
of plain light fresco
exclamations

plain light window
is all rectangle and books
for class lead to stairs
of painted lips
Lewinsky beret
heaven ice cream girls
in their geometric solace

skirt in a private collection
land in the still crossed arm light
street of limbs and packages
that's texture's planted foot
ascending to the town
where a sea-green curtain
waves goodbye until I appear

Baudelaire Poem

The rueful assorted ants author the moist
tall mice in great detail, majestic pain

A woman passes who with one hand
hooks the festival of the balconies
about us.
This house leans like a sea of gifts
to praise the statue.
I raise the lid on an extravagant
day for earless heads
to disgrace color, that one

A pastry filled with night, fugitive bread,
give my regards to the theater operator

Hill towns, marks of icy now,
Toes carved out of butter
melting in the thousand degrees
that ring cities

High-rise dust you keep escaping
with its pencil marks on winter light
expiration date
derision yes I will come
to your antique house
and remake myself

Job Titles

Dishwasher

this moment feels post-bathos,
wet-haired, nudged
to exhaustion
keep clapping, you'll arrange
the bridge, the tennis whites
scream lemonade. Ugly language
through the nose leads
me to keep track of names,
talk to everyone with money,
pay the price for blurb,
etc.

Jazz musician

begin to unroll your neighbor's
                              sleeves
the knots saturated by requests
to ignore evidence, history,
the chain of questions
that stretch from the sun
to your phobic kaleidoscope

Chinese Poet

            and an angry one
            that cascades from rock
            to ripe pocket of
            I will not call again
this grief has no pine
no bamboo, no thousand
grasses weeping with dew.
It's barefoot, a giant
record in a cave.

Unfinished Song

I dreamed about a song
and its promise to be you
as you sang with
many pennies, as you
said sunset is
the flowered sky—
I am keeping November in my collar.

(Print the film as soon as you can)

Cassette tape hopes
in Harvard Square.
How is the song carried?
Music . . . the door
for brisk reunions.

(Consistent menus over time)

Pie is a sensation
groped right away.
We sing the munificent
loss in our handbags,
answers to hurt the divan,
sorbet sensible champagne,
claw out a fashionable
tent for reunions.

You'd like onion soup to perfume everything
and I'd like to wear it. So create the bowls.
They'll feel unknown,
rigged from yarn to keen
your birthday.

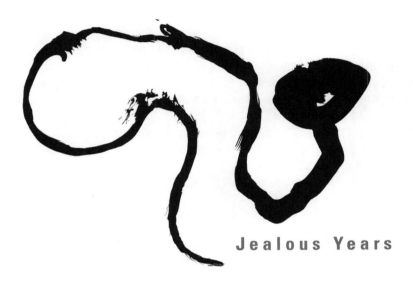

Jealous Years

I Can't Stand the City as I Saw It That Day

I heard about the sun
not only that it moved
but that it was mad,
as I would be
having been pushed to burn and burn
wandering over the white flecked tops of the minute waves
for a whale to cry, "my brown body is as smooth and lithe
in the water as you know the issue of your bowels to be. I move more
rapidly and my skin is like velvet. I am large and present myself to the
touch." Be careful
and cry at the sun, "the moving glycerin is a vast, subsumed body,
casting a great eye upwards, as if in play."
Penned in close to the shore,
I was afraid for both sides of the equation.

      I know that you are unkind by the glitter of your scales, how they
hook into the spreading of the roads.
      Obviously from your mien, the thick sieve you use to separate the
glutinous mass, I suspected opacity, times being what they are,
to fall. That's it. The way you sift. On a blur, I suspect everyone to be the
same.

"Oh, they've been kinder to that form."
Watch it bounce in, and now
all are smiles. "It's sweet."

What interesting black light effects with the lips

and how are the teeth!

Old leaves,
the water is boiling.
You will serve the same receptors where they always are.

From the shake of your hands
to your crown, proud display of cityscapes
that harmonize with this neighborhood's portion of sky.
Poolside,
exquisite choice, those statues.
How hard the adamantine doors
one must scratch to escape
and so be borne on a sea of blood,
unknown to the knuckles,
whose jealousy was of a higher sort.
There is one who sits in judgment.

Desire-reneger,
I have conquered your foothills
using crampons,
avoiding the intentional difficulties
proposed for our increasingly conquered globe.
I peer into the regions of perpetual mist
without much success. These rigors
are sustained by a whole class of people
working at our behest. Would that it snow
more freely, and the plastic wrapped
nudge each other in despair.

An engine and a siren
in an obscure academy. One day the fence was breached
by grunters, solid in their footsteps and knapsacks.
The lights are coming and we must run
and cast ourselves beneath the wheels.

In the housing there's a lot of spinning, but at last, it's dark.

Remember me by a shoelace that fastened you to your bicycle.

There, where bones and skulls are made anew
mon semblable,
sharp blade,
delightful scalpel, to wrest from your back
the way the bones move.

In the beginning, he cut between parts
but later found the spaces already there
shorn of resemblance.

Stinging tears and the move of a starfish for the water,
who drifts in the bright sun, we stopped above a sandbank
far from the shore, unplaceable to any lighthouse
though it was highest noon, and the sun played into the depths,
as you are, hair underwater

Ears of the Field

The leaves sign to the train tunnels,
"by your soldered doors we rest
from the noise and the light."

Between the two ears of the field lay the gate
above the urn of lies.
The fire hardened earth around the mouth
wide enough for one mouth
to talk with its lips
the lip language in the dark
that blinks: rundown dock,
you're the stitched indigo
and brass moment of the pulling street;
this is the fireman's clasp on the present friction
and all is wrapped in green
harangues of the dark hill

look again, both ways

where I wore a watch on each wrist
slow for the old face
and fast for all the new
and one watch died and was planted
in a hole
and we moved after the watch
up to the depth of an elbow

We Didn't Turn Over That Stone for Nothing

Not written down
and not done, but saved
by having enough memory.
Old frilly pants at ankle level,
do you like the thought
of my face a millimeter above the carpet
considering photographs?
The molding by the bathroom fan certainly works.
Pleasant hum. I would eat off most of the floors.
Angles touch me. The warm light through fabric,
a good sense of dry powders, kept well.

My cheek imprinted with the texture
Remembering your exciting back stairs
The nail bent to one side. Passing,
the tour took shape.
But your skin bothers me
when it blurts out around the house,
this can be torn as easily as a spider's web.

If a body meet a body
coming through the rye

Lessen the first body
by the other's falling
stamping a foot
in the same hall
moved by the hall out into the night
the rails wet
close like highway wires
after a rest stop
thinking again of the words formed.
Enhancing the plain, they
drain into a cistern, backed up
insect wings fly off the dash.

Grey Sky

Grey skies
old ritual
downwind
mine
most of valor
she raised
presumably
the creature runs
do not
over saucers
shortened to mean

Her Feet from Bone

vomit in public squares
race horses
in your cap and
possession
and spitting
herself
anxious as
and the words
turn themselves out
and your hand
yes

Winter Maid

In this	nothing
old cages	wrap their hearts
in snow	and the bicycle wishes
outlaw	veils
yes	symphony
tender	sentient
beaten	from corn
time	prevails

The Way the Bridge Folds Up

I wind my way home
trying to make my steps as steep as the hill,
bunch of trees at the bottom
lurks the old leg swept
aside by the storm,
hollows a deeper mark
before the road.

Hands, birds, and snow
freed from a branch.

Presented on a bridge,
box is a leap in the dark,
"Box Containing the Sound of Its Own Making."
He fell asleep. She was about to put it away
but checked again.

> To approach value
> lash the lines as X's
> the verticals following
> paths specified by the larger figures.

I'm sorry. Still she eats the hand,
her hair snatching at her neck, yellowed teeth
in the mail.

> Still she eats the hand,
abutting the bed with a grasp of theory,
her hair shorn of meaning.

You know the old bridge,
how people leave changed
stumbling into the pushed air,
lapse away the hand
uncovers the eyes.

45

Another Visit

I

I approach Tallinn with one arm blackened,
held out in front.
"He broke rocks for a living,"
then gathered around the peat fires
telling stories.

I approach Tallinn with one arm.
        The district of telephone poles barely visible
wrenching the soiled curtains in my direction
I tell you the stone was intended.

The houses back away from the street

and nothing is, not

brick chopping a field in various directions,

nor the windows, more scattered, poorer directions

given offhand, away from the aircraft carrier.

I approach the district where drunk Russian soldiers
act out the myth of Rudolf rushing the blood to their extremities.

II

In an apartment behind the triple-locked iron-banded doors
tea is served, "and if I had a little jam,
I would mingle it with the black bread you so fantastically acquired.
        Oh, those cigarettes!"
Your lovely hands as clever as the bone
washed beach where I throw my bottles
to break or be washed away as they like.
The water smooth the glass cuts
the sense out of the feet
                        and the name
                        buckles the
                        first flight of stairs
                        tacked to my mind
                        as I open the door
                        like the lapel smoothed
                        tradition of dust stuck.

Was I thinking that the statue would be you?

Snow Banks

Neck rotates on
the easy phrase
point of cloth

Bolts of it
sand before tread
an older color
hurries from the smoke

We'd sample causation
from the brown spine of a book

lead curve
silk bolts

waste twist white
blankets

debts forgiven

Equally Balanced Buckets

Play description: The imagination is inflamed by the other. The first letters of the alphabet meet. Trees weep. The shoreline, rocks, and hills are less comfortable than a martini-clad living room. But where do you expect the elemental embrace? Equally Balanced Buckets is a conversation about what you are thinking.

(Both A and B are on stage apart from each other.)

A: I killed the moment already.

B: Obviously, do you like my hat?

A: I like your question. It implies . . . well . . . that I could please you with compliments.

B: When in fact it is I who please you by drawing your compliments.

A: I thought of the perfect rejoinder.

B: What?

A: Neh, neh, budda, budda, budda . . . dismiss the paleontologist!

B: Oh yeah, 'cause I was saying . . .

A: About our fossils, imbedded in the question, the model for a new society identical to the old.

B: Shoving aside?

A: What would you give me?

B: Next week, problems, and it's not fair.

A: No, my weakness, from your timeline gathering folds of strength, like I was out in the garden and stopped.

B: You mean for a second?

A: No, just the dropped tomato plant, like I saw one of those cans with rust in it.

B: An opening circle,
   a lot of unused rainwater.

(A has moved close enough to B for B to grasp his arm.)

A: I thought that!
   Hold my arm here.

B: There's nothing separating it from your mind,
   just like last time with your fingers.

A: Snap fingers, see dandruff.

B: You're getting testy.

A: I didn't even have a tongue when you started talking.

B: Slight age difference. You noticed my hat. Notice now how I've removed it.

A: Some reminder.

B: Look, what are you afraid of?

A: Carrying water in equally balanced buckets to the well,
   one depends on the other.

B: What is this?

A: The world talking at me, "Here I am; I'm turning your way.
   Glance long at my lawns and hard at my fruit."

B: The dew, the dirt packed down.

A: Yes.

(Change of scene. B leaves. A either leaves or at least abandons the center of the stage to let C have her moment.)

C: My feet are cold like the blanket said.
My nose is older than my head.

Going out to fight over a paper bag
the message imbeds itself.

The tongue lags. A heel weighs
its soul. The chorus line portends
a future of kicks. A bucket drops
into a well. The scene resolves
into the seashore.

(A and C are not talking directly to each other. When C speaks, A may not even be able to hear.)

A: Rivulet to ankle, rivulet to ankle,
at last the formula alone: She can be any way she wants.
My own reply is selfishness. A thousand grains of sand
stick to my feet.

C: You've got to take flowers to market.
Your shoulders cry out.

A: Your eyes are balls of reason,
but removed before becoming a national dish.
I've been to the market and seen the cut flowers
hum a ballad of interdependency.

C: Your collar's raised like a wing.
You don't see or hear.

A: Senseless, but pushing my senses.
Farther down the beach I will find driftwood.
Driftwood, and free of the tangling seaweed.

(Change of scene: a meadow. A and C leave.)

B: I'm a woolgatherer. All knots fix me,
a poultice, a cockatrice, a temptress renewing
the sea, which is stormy, cloudy, gay with the intimations
of depths.
  Between the door and the window,
is the air I breathe.
  How my self is wrapped up with that robe. The rendition of
thought: she'll be coming round the cortex when she comes, she'll
be pullin', whaa, white horses when she comes. My skin changes.
A list of toenail-based reactions. A Welsh substitute. A lonely
hunting dog. Expensive Sami silver. The narrowing of cheek bones
near the North Pole. The color of eyes. The leaps of a kangaroo.
How well I know myself!
  The dry landscape renews before the research is completed.
Despite the facts, a long table sags. Before the first napkin's
unfolded I'm waving my hands.

(C appears with lambs around her.)

B: You've brought the pentimenti.
All of mine become faces.

(Change of scene: a room. B and C leave, A sits on a chair with a phone nearby.)

A: A telephone rings, you go down a rung,
a telephone rings, you go down a rung . . .

(A telephone rings.)

A: Yes?

(Silence)

A: Please speak, silence is boring.

Ahhh, you again, so long since . . . My oats, I'll dance a moment, hover with you over Damocles. How like the silver thread what I've heard through the earth. Crossing cities, the solitary Las Vegas reroutes my thoughts. A waterfall . . . but since you're listening, I'll finish.

After the canals we're dug Mars felt like any other planet. There was a place for it. Thought was extended to it. Color being no longer a problem, it was Venus metaphor reached. Mars shed its mythology, and the atmosphere escaped. The sky went dark at points surrounding the poles. Ice and dust formed there . . .

B: (from offstage, right away) **Read from another book.**

(C comes on stage and demonstrates the passing of time by ripping pages out of a calendar. C leaves and A and B come on stage.)

B: You're already here.

A: Yes, of course—I'll continue: so now it's like a dwelling; hair clogs the drains; the air from part one turns into heat in another; the garage door swallows you; and in succession the days . . .

B: Enough of this please. I'd like to be locked away in a cupboard, ignorant of the work ahead, or on a stool, with my paw a rough universe.

A: No details match the philosophy you turn me to, one where the proportions are all corrected.

Once out in a forest I noticed a tree and all its branches finished the job. They became lines to link ranks on a ridge while the light in my eye . . .

B: Squeeze it out of yourself. Come here.

A: For a long time, the little trees jumping around?

B: I don't know.

A: What is it? Factories have worked and stopped along rivers. Cars have lined up to receive the sun. Their aerials betoken unison, home at the end of the road—over the hill, beneath the pause—whatever your involuntary muscle desires.

B: What about your philosophy?

A: I like it when you bring me to that level. I admit it is about will. And the torn scarf of knowledge, whoever grabs it lags behind, and is granted that additional clarity—even me.

B: Have you . . .

A: Seen anything?
    "They wished they had a thousand eyes to gaze upon each other."
    I try to understand you. A beach stretches endlessly, with your hand trailing in the water. You are of the greatest or the smallest size. The ocean is a fever you are in or float above. Then we slosh off felicity to make directions out of the stars and feel the waves are navigational instruments.

B: And you try to wash your feet but there is still more sand before the car. Expectation is sealed in a glass by near physical laws. Can you see the contours of my face harden?

A: What a short thread your affirmation swings on . . . all the cocoons are memory spun. This pothole in your voice
    tells me about the night. Intense feats
    of jealousy remain.
    Your hairs measure the age
    when glasses laugh. The camel is back,
    dirty in your country.

B: The first night was so destructive to knowledge.
     You're in a chamber. The stars pass.
     The plan unfolds for you to have your own clock
     whisper yes yes yes I love it
     out of proportion.

A: And with the cantankerous
     zeal of the forest
     there is no light!
     Your hands are mentionable.
     I earn my reflection from talking.

     Air with a hundred fingers
     saying all hours
     create opportunity. Read that book
     and find that paper seals the roads
     in a ring of fond worry. The seals
     should listen. They're enough
     to talk at you passionately
     saying the road is time.
     Red rugs in the window again.

(C joins them on stage and gets the final word.)

C: The lambs take to the road. The flagstone laughs a concordance.
     Velvet is the wave, tamed by the contours of a couch. And in the
     sling of feeling a stone whirls.

The Original Lyric

Rome Again

Night's volumes:
known building, known building, known building,
cobblestone ends.

The link is a purse and a river.
By the river I wanted to steal a purse.
There was a dirty stream inside me.

On the circus floor,
I miss you, jug of wine.
On the banks
no expansive bridges
a nudge to find cracks free of needles
sententious flat appraisal.

As a layer slows history
or a horse is weight of bronze
to return by car in a stream of lights,
another conclusion.

Would You Take It from Me?

would you wrap it up please,
                          singing, a black cloak
toasts and the raw applause
                          and the flower
sticks in my neck.

You know the way the hands fall
                                and all
the fucking time was bitter if I tried.
And you know the glass, broken in the night.

Take a few steps, mincing the dark, the dew and
the expansion of the trees. Fell sheets of hours.
One more breath of the air
easy,
          I was against her neck.

And this the audience
couldn't see: A modern play,
They don't turn on the lights

Sometimes There Are Singing Threads Unbidden

My world unbidden,
closeted uproar of the veins
circle the stomach of a doubt.
Wrenched supple we were turning vast
locks ships mysteries the upper decks
(some beating roped off my heart)

Stuck to the roof of my mouth
I was going to.

Take certain steps like teeth wrenched,
vise for the juicy yesterday

give me the harvest of an old autumn
all fruits dropped to seed and none were stored,
nor were taken back, nor was I
put to seed,
                          nevertheless
autumn running rich the grass scorched fingers
for a cheek and the curve how many,
how many do you know
the times and ways, and how well?

was yesterday kept,
Upright on a lonely beach

Answer Sunken Patterns with a Raw Applause

       each cascading back to light the pitted forms of
females meeting making me.
Rubber I am rubber glove, floating just beyond
the stretching finger places. I was
turning them in my mind

was rich summer breaking mind

Wanting more this autumn especially,
those hands, long shadows longer now.
Open pink shells to hear the sea,

was bathing me,

When I came up with flesh and sat seaward
Plucking ships off the horizon, useless
but for those moments touching me

Stuff

When I reach up to pull some things and the shelf
with its irregular assortment of requests
is pulled by someone of my height,
I know that I will be asked again.

When someone of my height stands up
and the shelf in its shelved nature
is where my head was going,
of course everyone is woken up.

Dusting is all I'm doing now, but maybe
smashing that old pickle jar
would answer more completely,
                                        certain stirrings
for which I have assembled objects
that might not be worth the trouble.

After all, bringing them home is not the problem.

-17° C

Let the snow fall
because it's white
wind whisperer of halos
smirched and restless

A happy reunion
with coats maybe shouting
and hauled off rosy cheeks
special grip uneven hanging
the best trees
sharing the crazy tilt

(then the truth)
This because
Laughing is so unexpected
I hardly know when to shut up.
Don't gauge me by my happiness
I might not feel bad shoving my hand
down there after all
what's frosting
a swirl that brushes off

My snow not so easy
Caked and shifting
(what)
Shut up!
The skaters' circles even wider

Train Ride

I

A train ride I took once
where the rhythm of houses leaked
news of twilight's place.
The humming engine wanted back
its piston more,
trees than
cars we raced
right angles.

The problem with train rides at evening:
my proposal for shaking space into
sensory touching.
Evening's general problem expressed
succinctly by Dr. FiveAM,
too early,
for you to be wondering where your next breast
is coming from. Go on, give the homeless man
the Chinese food. Press your face to
the window approaching the city
on a train.
                    Jackrabbit of sky in a darkening
muscle twitch.
Turned up pud of a moment, filthy really,
this glass. Twice as many
chances to check your meaning.

Trees,
Throw away silhouettes riveted spasm down
by the steady clacking
list of movements best defined
by those guys with shovels
in coal rooms.

Ego sum game played
trains with myself hardly
checked steam boiler and the type
of schedule that ends
at 5:13.

II

New city for a gesture
Walked swiftly to the shining march
Fought science fiction
Hunkered after rest, this charming mind-shifting habit
promised to uphold,

        The night is lovely in its heat downtrodden
        Heat of night beautiful underfoot

        The night is often talked about
        To the night many times speech

        I cry the night away
        I to the night cry finish

        Night is black
        Night is black

Hardly matters, so is ink,
and there are dishes made with it.
            Marrow shoved to the side.
If only everything needed to be eaten.

Looking at a Batik

There is no gyration
or organized hum, these parts
cock at the elbow with readiness upon their face
huge cast shadows
in the pricked lattice of elaborate hair
and lurch.
When you see an overweening shadow
lurch at the crone's amazement at her pointed chin.

Across from a smaller number of heroes
whose sway is so much less.
They have the music to bump
the little moves of limbs
                        into a pattern, a night
throne of an opening,
a whole fantasy herded delicately past.

The screen.
The elaborate holes.
The fine shadow.

My thinking wrong.
For where I saw two groups of figures, there are two groups
and
no horizon,
the background black and placement
as of a chopping block
lolling this way and that among the cabbages
useless scrape
but where the figures are. Oh I don't
care about such things—they are
giants and they are heroes and
they all look like women.

Missing for You

We're kept in the sun until it's ready
to have a bare cupboard, a horn
for each hour. Look at the dusky air
pleasing streets,
you in them,
overly shod and forlorn,
made out of hair.

From the fruit trees crept a line of unreason.
In my dream those feet were silent parts.

In each instance
teeth are back in the shark's mouth.
That's why we drink,
to swallow,
and from some eaves
in the elbow pathways
Sie ist eine Klage
She is a lament.
Do you know more
about dusk-birth under bridges?

Wasps made you listen
to the tourniquet nonsense
of creation in mirrors and handouts.

It was the gorgons' softening of failure
when the earthworm sat and waited
and winter promised to be slow.
Your system is demolished.
I stood outside and kept the air silent.

Secrets on Call

Unbuttoned Forever

we can't imagine all the delight
in the scenery that you touched
I want to say troubadour neck
glass of derision
heels spotted with dew
lines in a stone suitcase
that was the feeling
driving in silence

Animadversion

You rented your hands and agreed.

This late morning my breath quickened as I strode, if you
can call it that, across grass.

I got down behind those metal shades and stayed even
when the dog scratched and pitifully. I read right through the
night, trying to sleep on the marble and on my bed, released
by birds finally when it was too late, and the thought of Coke
bottles kept me in love with the day I was going to miss.
That vacation . . .

You always smell like ear wax.
In my nightclothes the alien leader gesture
managed to unwrinkle
more skin than went into my umbrella,
telescope, mouth of patterns
to block the sun.

In my dream where I walked
the wind was a steady
interior doggerel
that made the picked fruit decay
before it sweetened.

The teeth I kept in rows
for fortune haggard mate
outlined the city where I would live,
much as I loved it, on my back only
and pressing the invitation to mice
to eat what I do not enjoy.

Unbelievable Arrows

In the believable pension
I cracked an egg
to tell your fortune
in water

The horses stopped improvising
on the beach

Jettison your offal burrows
            for once
I've taken the dreaming self
into a swimmer's kiss
The neck is one white sheet

and my rainy day
plans on a shelf

fingers in retreat

and her feet laughing
at the undertow

The Institutional Name for Nightwalking

You're coming up the fire escape and
the cars are ready in the dark
before the plane flies
beating snow dirty, back into silence.
In the city they wear hats and direct traffic.

And I remember how *On the Road*
name dropped and made something out of your
twenties and unfolded in a kitchen wood,
glass and worn floor silence. And then
in Chinese where we did have string beds
I slept in the afternoon preparing
for that persimmon.

But I digress. There's an end-of-the-year dark where
the clouds mean it's all water and rocks and
you run against the rules staining the concrete pebbles
with drippings from your shorts

Another Letter

How are your neighbors, the feeble-minded men?
Do they soothe with their eye flashing through the foliage
as they approach the fence
swinging the lamps that will not be lit again
in our lifetime?
Do you buckle to the earth
its yawning and your yawning
the swing of the chandelier
distracting animal movement?
I imagine that when the drawbridge
on your bed raises
you are one with the sheets,
tangled in a good way
as you fall.

My lips and teeth and tongue feel dry all night.

Do you approach sleep
hand-in-hand with your sheets
blanking out in the midst of the circle
amused lips pulled back by the wind?

I came out of the woods as the sun dropped.

The thick ropes of muscle are really water
where the shoulders grasped are barrels.
You don't understand the party.
Is your dog's tail slicked back
by your mind that quinces round
behind glasses? Why rot
when there are shambling silences
distending like nature film tongues?

Miserable fun:
a dog's bark comes across my face
resetting the yes again
as cigarette covers the space.
Not that it's bad river ambles
to plump the cushions,
but I think it is
unwilling to change.

Though the hills are already denuded
we left the land
so I might meet you.
Will you topple monuments
into my lap, raising the level of those pools
they have in front of temples?

Don't stick your tongue out because I know the words.
I won't go on into the bric-a-brac
as if I understood their odd shadows
ringing out over the unfurled land
that I came to in my later years.

Holiday Spirit

Snow is a teacher, a billion stars agree,
and shave
the consequences
from wrapping gifts, much as I
love temporal treasure
it's a cold ball.

And the voice signals
no catches in your arms
the pirate's standard
says yes
your cap has the spirit.
I'm in clothes of welcoming yarn
itemizing my shadowy pleasure,
the same that kept me shod.

Then we swim
in the reprobate slicing and dicing
up the turkey's neck. I had a parcel of feathers
that I glued to my face
to remove skin for the needle, my ears
not even pierced I did center the part
on my scalp that you claimed.

MERITAGE PRESS PROJECTS

(since 2001)

"Cold Water Flat" (2001). Signed and numbered etching by Archie Rand and John Yau. Limited edition of 37.

100 More Jokes From The Book of the Dead (2001). A monograph documenting a collaboration between Archie Rand and John Yau.

er, um (2002). A collection of ten poems by Garrett Caples and six drawings by Hu Xin. Limited edition of 75 copies. Signed and numbered by the poet.

Museum of Absences (2003). Poetry collection by Luis H. Francia. (Copublished with the University of the Philippines Press.)

Opera: Poems 1981-2002 (2003) by Barry Schwabsky.

Veins (2003). A poetry broadside by David Hess.

[ways] (2004). A poetry-art collaboration between Barry Schwabsky and Hong Seung-Hye. (Copublished with Artsonje Center, Seoul.)

The Oracular Sonnets (2004). An e-publication of a visual poetry collaboration between Mark Young and Jukka-Pekka Kervinen.

PINOY POETICS: A Collection of Autobiographical and Critical Essays on Filipino and Filipino-American Poetics (2004). Edited by Nick Carbo.

Meritage

Press

Sean Finney is a poet, journalist, and copywriter living in San Francisco. He was born farther west, in Hawaii, but likes to claim that Rome, where he lived as a teenager, is his spiritual home. This is his first book. His Web site is **www.stfinney.com**.

Ward Schumaker is a San Francisco based illustrator who has illustrated two books for the acclaimed Yolla Bolly Press: *Paris France* by Gertrude Stein, and *Two Kitchens in Provence* by M.F.K. Fisher. His Web site is **www.warddraw.com**.